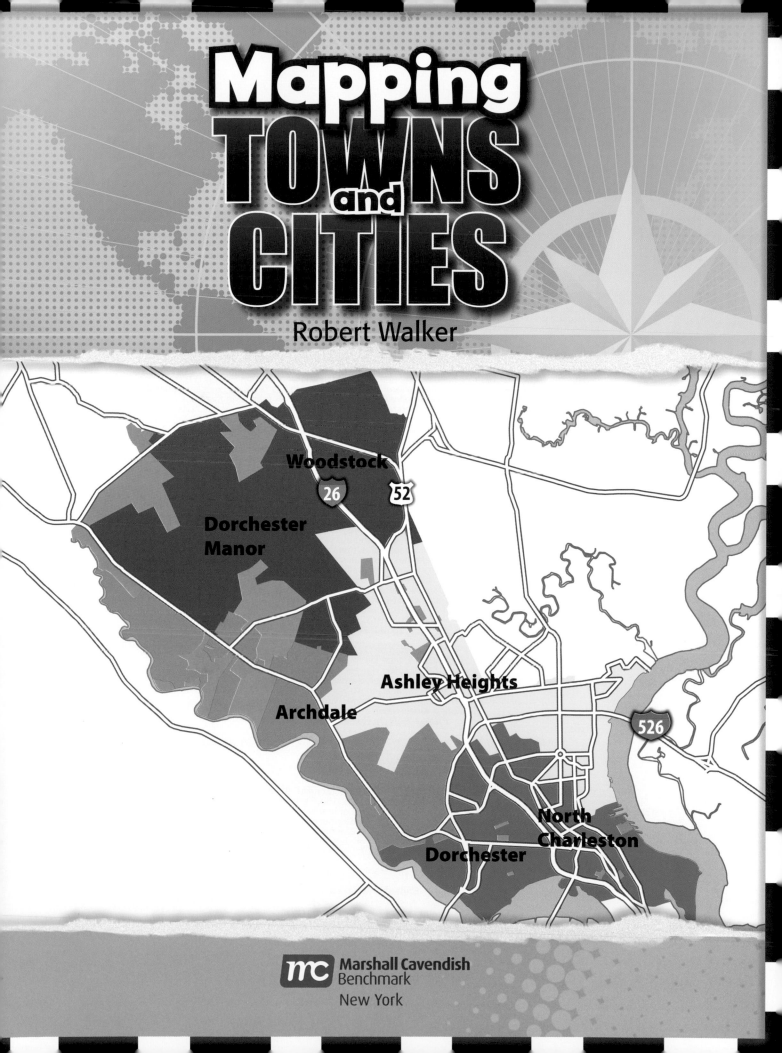

# Mapping
# TOWNS and CITIES

### Robert Walker

**Marshall Cavendish**
Benchmark
New York

This edition first published in 2011 in the United States
by Marshall Cavendish Benchmark.

Marshall Cavendish Benchmark
99 White Plains Road
Tarrytown, NY 10591
www.marshallcavendish.us

Copyright © 2011 Q2AMedia

Published by Marshall Cavendish Benchmark
An imprint of Marshall Cavendish Corporation

Other Marshall Cavendish Offices:
Marshall Cavendish International (Asia) Private Limited, 1 New Industrial Road, Singapore 536196 • Marshall Cavendish
International (Thailand) Co Ltd. 253 Asoke, 12th Flr, Sukhumvit 21 Road, Klongtoey Nua, Wattana, Bangkok 10110,
Thailand • Marshall Cavendish (Malaysia) Sdn Bhd, Times Subang, Lot 46, Subang Hi-Tech Industrial Park,
Batu Tiga, 40000 Shah Alam, Selangor Darul Ehsan, Malaysia

Marshall Cavendish is a trademark of Times Publishing Limited

Library of Congress Cataloging-in-Publication Data
Walker, Robert.
Mapping towns and cities / by Robert Walker.
p. cm. — (Mapping our world)
Includes bibliographical references and index.
Summary: "Introduces maps and teaches essential mapping skills, including how to create,
use, and interpret maps of towns and cities"—Provided by publisher.
ISBN 978-1-60870-120-9
1. Cartography—Juvenile literature. 2. Maps--Juvenile literature.
3. Cities and towns--Juvenile literature. I. Title.
GA105.6.W353 2011
912'.19732--dc22
2010002035

Created by Q2AMedia
Series Editor: Deborah Rogus
Art Director: Harleen Mehta
Client Service Manager: Santosh Vasudevan
Project Manager: Kumar Kunal
Line Artist: Achinto Chatterjee, Narinder Kasana
Coloring Artist: Nazia Zaidi, Shweta Singh
Photo research: Rajeev Parmar

The photographs in this book are used by permission and through the courtesy of:

Cover: Space Imaging/NASA
Half title: Joe LeMonnier

4-5: Adam Kazmierski/Istockphoto; 6: Joe LeMonnier; 7: Joe LeMonnier; 8: Joe LeMonnier; 9t: Hulton Archive/
Getty Images; 9b: Joe LeMonnier; 10t: Richard Klotz/Istockphoto; 10b: Terry Wilson/Istockphoto; 12: Joe LeMonnier;
13t: Joe LeMonnier; 13b: Chad Bontrager/Shutterstock; 14: Joe LeMonnier; 16: Iofoto/Shutterstock; 17t: Joe LeMonnier;
17b: 2010 Valley Ride; 18t: Tomas Woff/Shutterstock; 18b: Stephen VanHorn/Shutterstock; 20: Joe LeMonnier;
21t: Frank Siteman/Photolibrary; 21b: Joe LeMonnier; 22: Joe LeMonnier; 23: Joe LeMonnier; 24: Nikitsin/Shutterstock;
25t: Andrew Buckin/Shutterstock; 25b: Joe LeMonnier; 26t: Joe LeMonnier; 26b: Charlie Hutton/Shutterstock;
28t: MVRDV; 28b: NASA; 29: Fotomak/Shutterstock

Q2AMedia Art Bank: 11, 15, 19, 27

Printed in Malaysia

1 3 5 6 4 2

# Contents

Words in **bold** are defined in the Glossary.

# Bright Lights, Big Cities

Do you live in a city or town? If you live in the United States, there's a good chance you do. More than 80 percent of people in this country live in a city or **suburb**. That's almost 250 million people!

## Where It All Happens

Cities and towns are the world's hotspots for **culture**, entertainment, industry, and business. The movies and TV shows we watch, the clothes we wear, and many of the **products** we use are made in big cities and towns. Cities like New York and Tokyo, Japan, are home to huge companies, professional sports teams, museums, theaters, and millions of people.

New York City is the largest city in the United States. It is home to more than 8 million people.

# Why Map Towns and Cities?

How do you plan a community, build it, and keep it running? Maps! People called city planners use maps to decide where to build, and they make maps that show how water, electricity, and gas will get to all the people who live there. City planners even map out routes for garbage collection and public transportation. Once a city is built, maps also help people get from one place to another, whether they're traveling by foot, train, subway, bus, bike, or car.

## Did You Know?

The three largest cities in the United States are New York City, Los Angeles, California (3.8 million), and Chicago, Illinois (2.9 million). More people live in these three cities than in the states of Maine, New Hampshire, Vermont, Connecticut, Massachusetts, and Rhode Island combined!

# Reading Maps

Maps provide all kinds of information. For example, some maps show the **population density**, school and business zones, and bus routes. Maps can also show you how to get around town.

## Using Map Tools

Even though there are many different types of maps, most maps have certain elements, or features, in common. By learning to use these features, you can read almost any map.

**COMPASS ROSE**
A compass rose shows the orientation of the directions: north, south, east, and west.

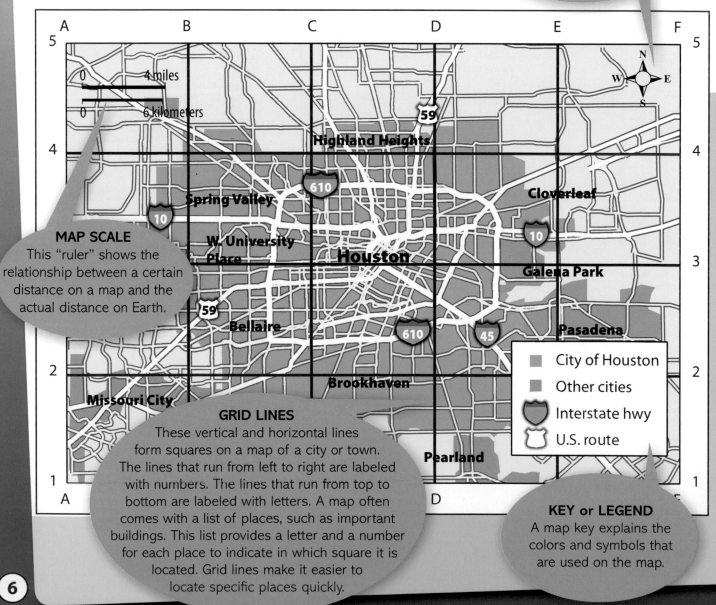

**MAP SCALE**
This "ruler" shows the relationship between a certain distance on a map and the actual distance on Earth.

**GRID LINES**
These vertical and horizontal lines form squares on a map of a city or town. The lines that run from left to right are labeled with numbers. The lines that run from top to bottom are labeled with letters. A map often comes with a list of places, such as important buildings. This list provides a letter and a number for each place to indicate in which square it is located. Grid lines make it easier to locate specific places quickly.

**KEY or LEGEND**
A map key explains the colors and symbols that are used on the map.

Map labels: Highland Heights, Spring Valley, Cloverleaf, W. University Place, Houston, Galena Park, Bellaire, Pasadena, Missouri City, Brookhaven, Pearland

Key:
- City of Houston
- Other cities
- Interstate hwy
- U.S. route

# What Maps Can We Use?

There are many types of maps we can use to study cities and towns. The most common maps are thematic maps. Thematic maps provide information about a community, such as the location of tourist attractions or recreation areas. Physical maps show the elevation, or height, of the land, which helps planners know where to build. Road maps include the streets and highways. Transportation maps show things like bus and subway routes.

## Map It!
## What's in a City?

Political maps show how a city or town is divided into different sections. Political maps help us see the districts, **wards**, **townships**, and **boroughs** within a city.

## Read It!

Lines and colors are used to mark the sections of the city. The key explains what each color and symbol represents. How many zip code districts are in the city of Portland, Oregon?

# The First Towns

Ancient humans were hunter-gatherers who often moved from place to place in search of food. That all changed when people finally learned to farm—approximately 10,000 years ago. Instead of having to search for food, they could grow their own and set up permanent villages.

The first villages were settled on **fertile** ground near rivers, which were important for farming. A river also provided a means of transportation and a route to a sea or ocean, and it helped protect the community. By 3500 BCE, some villages had become highly organized cities and centers of **agriculture** and trade.

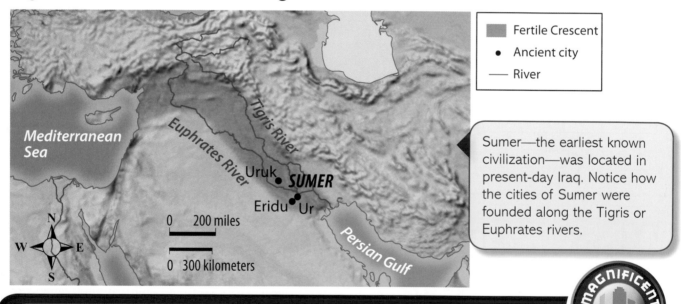

Fertile Crescent
● Ancient city
— River

Sumer—the earliest known civilization—was located in present-day Iraq. Notice how the cities of Sumer were founded along the Tigris or Euphrates rivers.

## Ancient Rome

The Roman Empire was one of the largest empires in history, but it wasn't always big. It began as small villages founded by farmers atop hills near the Tiber River, which flowed into the Mediterranean Sea. The first settlers chose the area because the hilltops provided safety from attackers and the river gave them access to fresh water, trade, and transportation. These separate villages slowly grew into one city that covered nearly 500 square miles (1,295 square kilometers). Rome (in present-day Italy) was the capital of the Roman Empire for more than seven hundred years.

# Location, Location, Location

Trade and travel routes were also likely places to settle a village or town. The reason was simple: people needed to buy and sell products from these traveling traders. London, England, was founded along the River Thames (pronounced "temz"), which flowed into the sea. It started as a tiny town, but by the 1500s it was booming. Londoners were making money trading fish, cloth, glass, and wine. Between 1530 and 1600, London's population tripled.

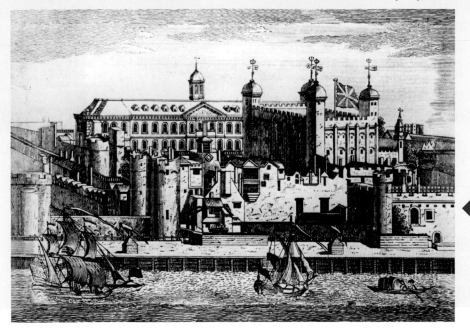

This image shows London during the 1600s. The River Thames ran through the center of the city. Many important buildings, such as the Tower of London, were built near the river.

# Resources and Industry

During the 1800s, whenever coal, iron, or gold was discovered, people rushed to the area hoping to strike it rich. Because miners needed goods and services, people opened stores and businesses, and the small mining settlements soon turned into towns. Eventually, factories that used the resources being mined opened near these towns, and even more people headed there to find work.

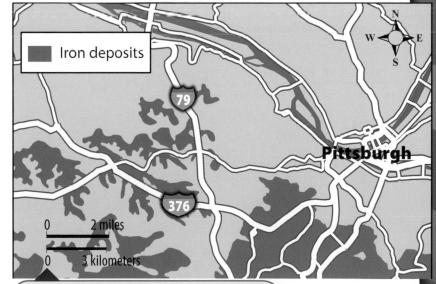

Iron deposits

Pittsburgh boomed after iron **deposits** were found in Pennsylvania. By 1911, it was the nation's eighth-largest city. The red areas show the metal deposits.

# Birth of the Suburbs

For centuries people moved to cities to find jobs. Soon cities became overcrowded, dirty, and expensive. During the twentieth century, some people got tired of dealing with the hassles of city-living. Many left and headed for greener pastures—the suburbs!

These smaller outlying communities offered less expensive housing and more space. Planners created maps to build highway systems, railways, and subways so that people living in a suburb could easily get to the city for work. The plans were a success. Each day millions of people in the United States **commute** from the suburbs to the city for work.

When suburbs were first built, almost all the houses looked the same, which made the planning and building of a suburb easier and less expensive.

MAGNIFICENT • TOWN •

## Mesa, Arizona

Mesa, a suburb of Phoenix, Arizona, has become the largest suburb in the United States. It is bigger than some major cities, including St. Louis, Missouri, and Miami, Florida. Mesa is 125 square miles (324 km²) in size, with a population of nearly 500,000 people. Why is Mesa so popular? It offers everything a major city does: museums, concert halls, golf courses, art galleries, and excellent schools.

# Activity

## Plan a Suburb!

A lot of planning goes into building a suburb! **Developers** use thematic maps to plan where to build houses, roads, and parks. Where will you put houses and streets in your suburb?

**Materials**
- blank piece of paper
- pencil
- colored pencils
- ruler

**1** Draw a large rectangle on a piece of paper. This area will be your new suburb.

**2** Decide where you want to locate the **downtown** and draw in businesses, shops, and restaurants. Use a different colored pencil for each. Label the downtown.

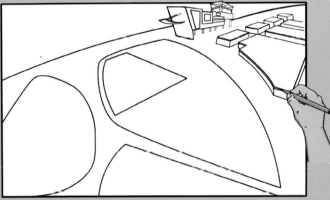

**3** Now decide where you want to put the residential area. Pick a colored pencil you have not used yet and draw in houses.

**4** Select another color and draw in some schools. Label the schools.

**5** Now draw in parks, ponds, or sports fields. Make sure to label them.

**6** Add some fun features, such as museums, movie theaters, or hiking trails.

**7** Complete your suburb by drawing in roads so that residents can get around town. Add traffic lights or stop signs.

**8** Make a key by drawing a box on your map. Be sure to include each color you used and write down what that color stands for on your map.

**9** Finally, name your suburb!

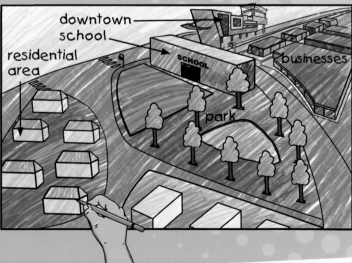

# Building Cities

How does a small town grow into a big city? Usually from the inside out! In medieval times the center of a city was a castle or fortress, and the city grew outward from there.

Today, most cities still follow this design. City planners locate the important government buildings and large businesses in the center.

## Grid vs. Wheel-and-Spoke

Look at a map of your city or town. If you live in a modern community, you'll probably see that the streets are laid out like a grid. This is the most popular plan for new cities and suburbs because it makes the most use of the land. It also makes getting around a lot easier!

Older cities, however, weren't quite as well planned. As the population increased, new buildings were put up on the edge of the city. Roads and streets were added to connect the new buildings to the city center. Government buildings and businesses were at the center, and the streets extended outward in rings and spokes. From overhead, a city that was built this way looks like a wheel.

Moscow

The Kremlin

**Moscow, Russia**
- Center city
- Red Square
- Park
- Roads

0    4 miles

0    6 kilometers

Look at the map on page 13. How are the layouts of Chicago and Moscow, Russia, different? Which city do you think would be easier to travel in?

# Neighborhoods and Districts

It is difficult to make sure a huge city runs smoothly. Some cities are divided into smaller sections that are easier to manage, such as townships, boroughs, wards, and districts. Many of these smaller communities are like little cities—some even have their own government offices and leaders. Breaking a city or town into smaller areas makes managing and running things a whole lot easier.

A city map show the ways a city or town is broken up into smaller sections. Then each section is mapped to give a close-up view.

## Chicago, Illinois

After the Great Chicago Fire in 1871, the city had to be rebuilt and replanned. Architects from all over the country came to the city. By 1885, Chicago was home to one of the first skyscrapers, and more followed. Chicago became an important center of trade, industry, and finance.

Today, Chicago is divided into four sections: the North Side, South Side, West Side, and Downtown, which includes the Loop. The city is planned on a grid system, and each section is divided into neighborhoods and wards. Chicago has more than 210 neighborhoods and is home to 2.9 million people.

**Chicago, Illinois**
- Chicago Loop
- Park
- "L" system trains

Chicago Ave.

Grand Ave.

Chicago River

LaSalle Blvd.

Chicago

Adams St.

S. Michigan Ave.

Lake Shore Dr.

Lake Michigan

41

Grant Park

0   0.4 miles

0   0.6 kilometers

This map shows downtown Chicago. The Loop—shown in dark orange—is the central business district downtown. Its name refers to the "L" (elevated) train circuit that surrounds it.

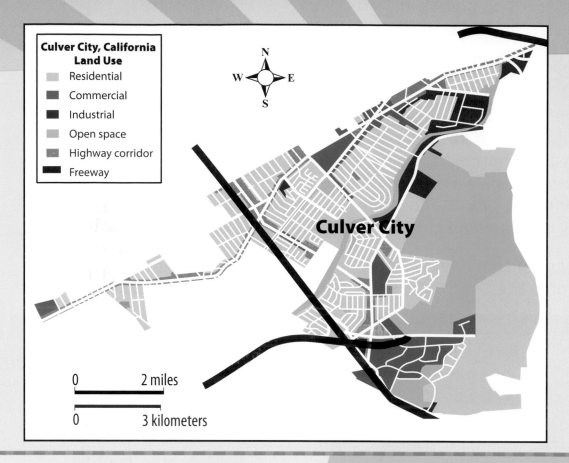

**Culver City, California Land Use**
- Residential
- Commercial
- Industrial
- Open space
- Highway corridor
- Freeway

N
W E
S

Culver City

0       2 miles

0       3 kilometers

## Map It! Where to Build

Cities and neighborhoods are planned so that big businesses are concentrated in one area and houses and recreation facilities are in other areas. When people want to build a house or factory, they have to make sure they are building in an area that has been **zoned** for that purpose.

## Read It!

Different colors are used to mark what land is meant for homes, public areas, businesses, and factories. If you wanted to build a house in Culver City, California, where could you build it?

## Starting Over

Maps don't just help people build a new city. They can help people rebuild, too. During World War II, European cities, including Berlin, Germany, and London, England, were destroyed by bombs. Maps helped people reconstruct their cities. How? If a whole block had been destroyed, people used **property line** maps to figure out where boundaries were before the war. Workers also used maps to find and repair the **utilities** underneath all of that rubble.

## Growing Pains

Growing isn't easy. In many cities, most of the available land is already being used. Maps can help developers figure out how to expand a city while still paying attention to things such as protected areas or natural obstacles. In Helsinki, Finland, developers are actually draining water from coastal areas so they have room to build. Today, there are huge areas of the city that used to be underwater!

# Activity

## Find Your Bearings

**Materials**
- piece of construction paper
- pencil
- piece of cardboard
- tape or paste
- ruler

Before mapping an area, workers survey the land. Surveyors measure the elevation of land features. They record the location, or bearing, of each feature in relation to the others. To do this they use a bearing board, which measures the angle between two locations. Angles are measured in degrees (°). You can make a bearing board and try measuring angles yourself!

**1** Trace the bearing board onto your piece of paper. Use your ruler to create straight lines from the hash marks to the center. Then extend all the lines to the edge of the paper.

**2** Label each line in 5-degree increments (5°, 10°, 15°, etc.). Put 360°/0° at the top and, going clockwise, label up 355°. Paste or tape your paper onto the piece of cardboard.

**3** Go outside and find two things to measure, such as your house and a nearby tree. Put your board on the ground facing them. Line up the 0° mark with the object on the left. Mark it on the cardboard.

**4** Keep the 0° mark pointing toward the left object. Then use the ruler to line up the object on the right. Make a pencil mark on the cardboard where the ruler is.

**5** How many degrees are between the two marks? This is the angle, or bearing, between the two objects.

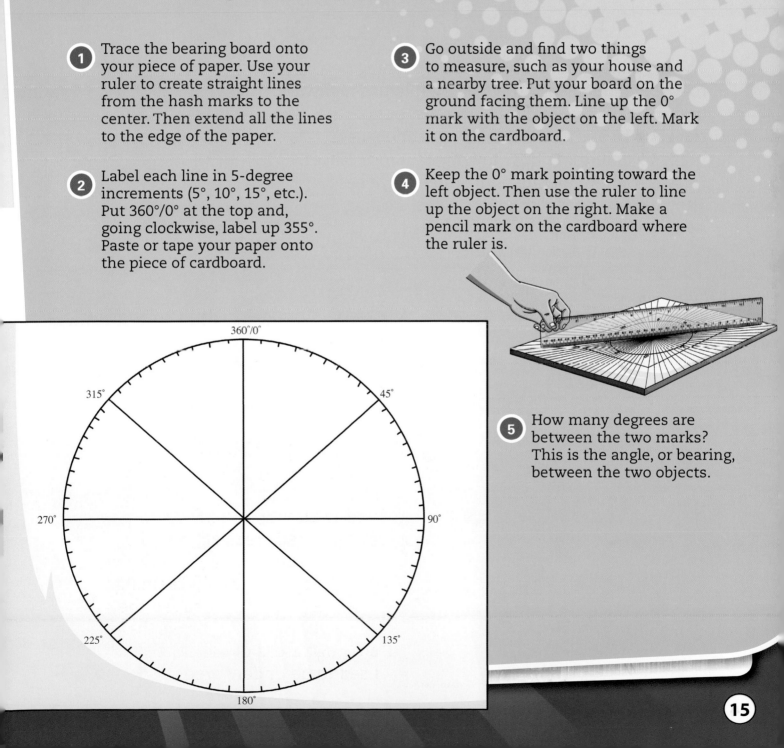

# From Here to There

Think of all the different ways people get around town—streets, highways, trains, subways, bike paths, and walkways. Maps are used to help plan and build all of these different types of transportation routes. Maps also help people use them.

## Streets and Highways

There's a lot to think about when building new roads. Planners study the way people use highways and roads to figure out where most people are traveling to and from. Then the planners use maps to determine how to connect those places. However, they can't just put streets anywhere. They have to consider historic sites, existing neighborhoods, and future city plans.

Los Angeles, California, is one of the United States' busiest places for road traffic. During the 1950s and 1960s, thousands of acres of land were used for building new roads.

# All Aboard!

City streets and highways are congested and crowded, which can make it hard to get around. To help cut down on all this traffic, city planners decided to build subways and **elevated** trains that would connect areas of the city.

At first these systems were pretty small—just a few stops right in downtown. Today, the rail systems in large cities can have many different lines, or routes. There are dozens of stops along each train line. You need to be able to understand schedules and maps so you get on the right train!

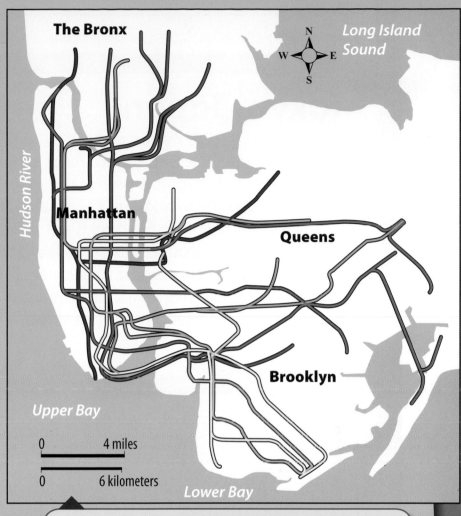

This map shows the subway lines in New York City. Travelers can ride the Green Line to get from the Bronx to Manhattan. Which lines go to Brooklyn? To Queens?

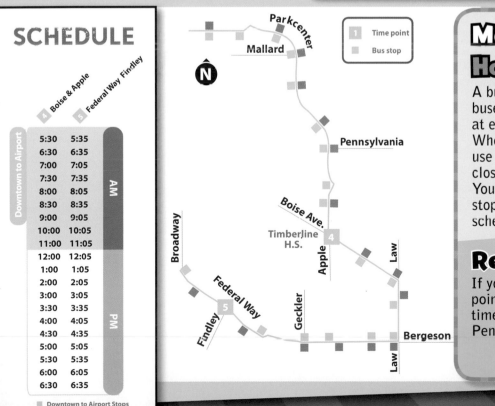

## SCHEDULE

| | 4 Boise & Apple | 5 Federal Way Findley | |
|---|---|---|---|
| **Downtown to Airport** | 5:30 | 5:35 | **AM** |
| | 6:30 | 6:35 | |
| | 7:00 | 7:05 | |
| | 7:30 | 7:35 | |
| | 8:00 | 8:05 | |
| | 8:30 | 8:35 | |
| | 9:00 | 9:05 | |
| | 10:00 | 10:05 | |
| | 11:00 | 11:05 | |
| | 12:00 | 12:05 | **PM** |
| | 1:00 | 1:05 | |
| | 2:00 | 2:05 | |
| | 3:00 | 3:05 | |
| | 3:30 | 3:35 | |
| | 4:00 | 4:05 | |
| | 4:30 | 4:35 | |
| | 5:00 | 5:05 | |
| | 5:30 | 5:35 | |
| | 6:00 | 6:05 | |
| | 6:30 | 6:35 | |

■ Downtown to Airport Stops

## Map It!
## Hop on the Bus

A bus map shows the times buses are scheduled to arrive at each stop along a route. When you take the bus, you use the schedule to find the closest time point to your stop. You need to arrive at that stop earlier than the scheduled time.

## Read It!

If you need to reach time point 5 by 7:35 a.m., what time should you be at the Pennsylvania stop?

# Tokyo, Japan

Approximately 12.8 million people are packed into the 848 square miles (2,197 km²) of Tokyo. It is one of the largest cities in the world and the **financial hub** of Japan. Trains and subways are the main ways to get around this crowded city. In fact, Tokyo has the largest subway and train system in the world! It's also one of the cleanest and most efficient systems.

## Did You Know?

Only the main streets in Tokyo have names. The smaller streets and roads don't have names or numbers!

## Talking Maps

Global Positioning System (GPS) is a navigational tool that uses **satellites** to find any point on Earth. GPS has changed the way people **navigate**—no more paper road maps! Many people can get directions right from their cell phones or from units in their cars. You just program where you are and where you want to go, and GPS technology does the rest! GPS units have screens that display the route so you can see your progress. Many devices actually "talk," telling you exactly where to turn.

# Activity

## Giving Directions

**Materials**
- map of a city (provided)
- colored pencils

You work at a tourist information center. It's your job to help people find their way around the city. Several people approach you, asking for directions. Remember, your job is to give them the easiest and most direct route.

**1** Photocopy the map. Using the map, draw the best route to each destination. Circle the destinations and use a different colored pencil to draw each route. When giving driving directions, circle the closest parking lot.

**2** The Allens want to spend a day in the park. The weather is nice, so they want to walk to the park. Along the way, they'd like to see the fountain.

**3** John is late for his sister's wedding. She is getting married at the local church. He needs to get there fast and park his car close by!

**4** Sarah and Mike want to see the dinosaur **exhibit** at the museum. Afterward, they want to go to dinner at a nearby restaurant.

**5** Billy's cat Socks is due for a check-up at the veterinarian's office. Billy doesn't have a car. He must walk or ride his bike.

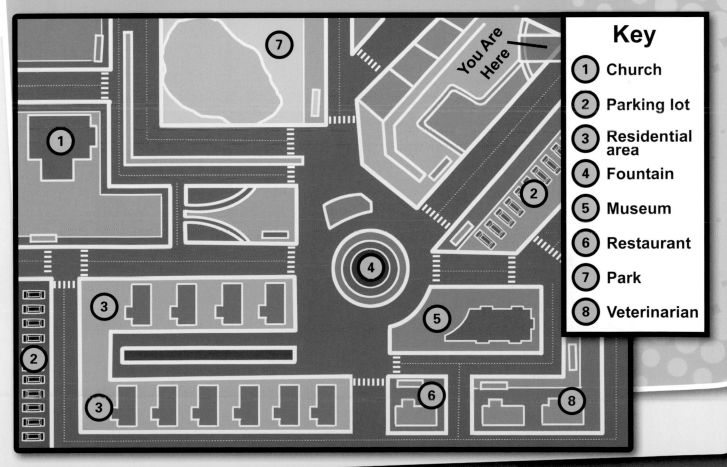

**Key**

1 Church
2 Parking lot
3 Residential area
4 Fountain
5 Museum
6 Restaurant
7 Park
8 Veterinarian

# Serving the City

Roads and buildings are what we notice most about a city. But there are other things that are just as important—even if we never think about them. What's so important? Utilities! We need utilities to provide electricity, gas, and water. We also need other services, like sewers, trash collection, hospitals, and schools. Maps help with the planning and maintenance of these important city services.

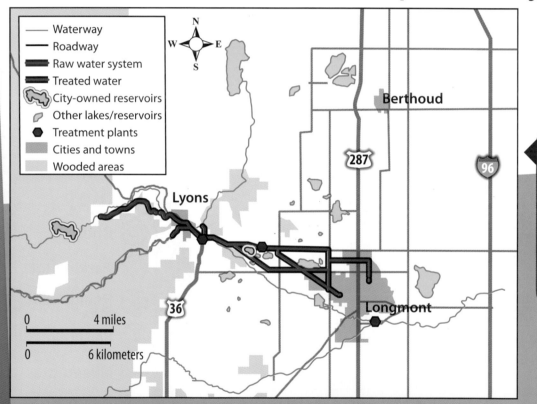

Waterway
Roadway
Raw water system
Treated water
City-owned reservoirs
Other lakes/reservoirs
Treatment plants
Cities and towns
Wooded areas

Berthoud

Lyons

Longmont

287
96
36

0    4 miles
0    6 kilometers

Most utility systems are underground. This map shows the water supply system for Longmont, Colorado. Look at the key. Find the pipes that are for treated water.

## Drinking It Up

When you turn on the faucet water comes out, but where does it come from? A system of underground pipes carries the water from treatment plants into houses and buildings. The treatment plants **filter** the water to make sure it is clean and safe to drink. Without maps, workers would not know where to build the pipes or be able to maintain them.

**Did You Know?**

The ancient Greeks and Romans were some of the first people to have plumbing.

# Powering the City

When electricity was introduced to cities in the late 1800s, planners had to figure out how to connect every building, house, and streetlight. In big places like Philadelphia, Pennsylvania, and Boston, Massachusetts, miles of power lines were strung up along poles. Workers used maps to plan the placement of power lines.

A system of power lines can be pretty complicated. Maps are used to keep the system running, fix problems, and add more lines.

# Keeping It Clean

Sewer, or sanitation, systems help keep cities clean and people healthy. Many early sewer systems drained into the street or into the same rivers from which people got their drinking water. During the mid-1800s, people started building underground sewer systems, and they used maps to figure out where to put and connect the pipes. These pipes and drains keep wastewater separate from drinking water—and off our streets!

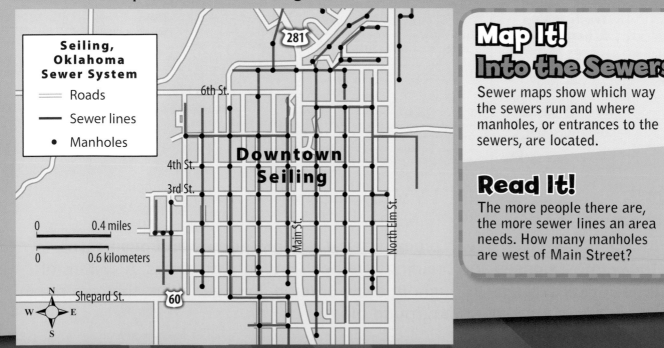

**Seiling, Oklahoma Sewer System**
- ═══ Roads
- ─── Sewer lines
- • Manholes

0 ———— 0.4 miles

0 ———— 0.6 kilometers

281

6th St.

4th St.

3rd St.

Downtown Seiling

Main St.

North Elm St.

Shepard St.

60

N W E S

## Map It!
### Into the Sewers

Sewer maps show which way the sewers run and where manholes, or entrances to the sewers, are located.

## Read It!

The more people there are, the more sewer lines an area needs. How many manholes are west of Main Street?

# Picking It Up

Trash collection is another important part of keeping a city clean. Trash collection wasn't always organized, which meant garbage often piled up in the streets. It was a street sweeper's job to sweep the garbage away.

Today, garbage is picked up every week. People use maps to divide the city, make schedules, and plan routes for collection. Maps and schedules help trash collectors do their jobs and make sure everyone's garbage and recycling are picked up on schedule.

## Did You Know?

In big cities like New York, workers pick up almost 23,000 tons (20,865 metric tons) of trash each day.

If you lived in Ashley Heights, what day would your garbage be picked up?

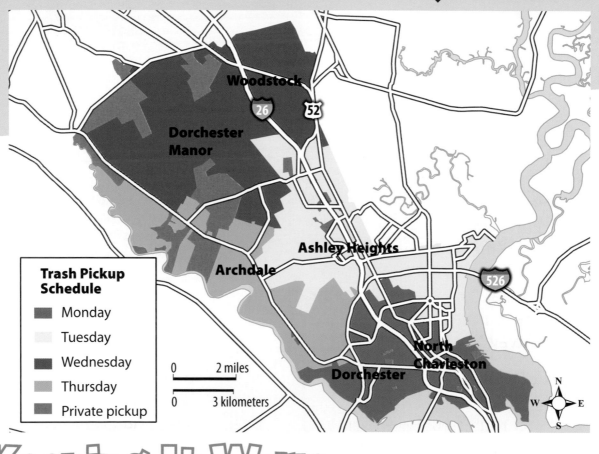

**Trash Pickup Schedule**
- Monday
- Tuesday
- Wednesday
- Thursday
- Private pickup

Woodstock
26  52
Dorchester Manor
Ashley Heights
Archdale
526
North Charleston
Dorchester

0   2 miles
0   3 kilometers

N
W   E
S

# Keeping It Warm

In the 1880s, cities began piping natural gas into homes and businesses. Today, most houses and buildings are heated with natural gas. A system of pipes distributes gas throughout a city or town. In larger cities, that can mean hundreds of miles of underground pipes.

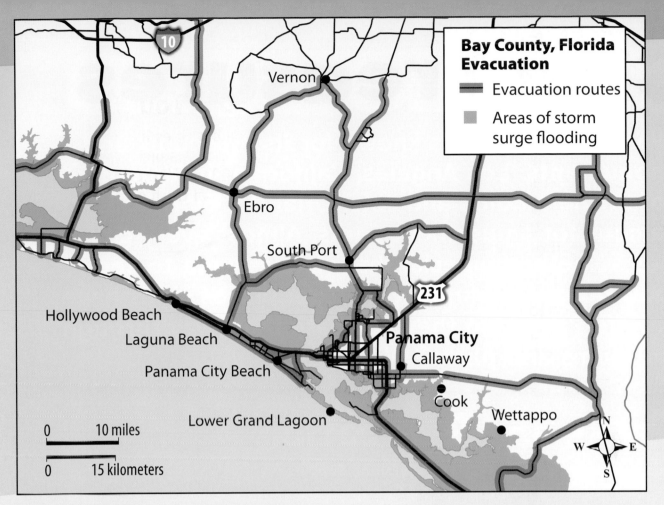

On this evacuation map for Bay County, Florida, the evacuation routes are highlighted in red. People should follow the route closest to their homes when leaving the city.

# Keeping Healthy and Safe

Have you ever seen a blue sign with a white *H* and an arrow on it? These signs point the way to the nearest hospital. Planners map the quickest and easiest route to a hospital. They then put up the signs along these routes so that people can find their way to a hospital.

Other types of planned routes are **evacuation** routes. City planners identify the most direct routes—usually main roads and highways—out of a city. Then they create special maps that show the evacuation routes so people can safely get out of town if there is an emergency or a big storm, such as a hurricane.

# Learning Zones

Many towns have more than one school. How do you know which one is yours? Maps are used to divide the city into public school districts and assign every student to a school. These maps also help the school officials plan bus routes for each school.

# City Treasures

Washington, D.C., is known for its museums and monuments. Los Angeles, California, is famous for movie studios and sets. Orlando, Florida, is famous for amusement parks. Almost every city has something special that visitors want to see. How do people find all the cool places cities have to offer? How do they navigate their way through museums and parks? With maps!

## Parks and Recreation

When planning a city, developers make sure to set aside land for parks so that people can enjoy the outdoors. Park maps show the features different parks have to offer, such as picnic areas, playgrounds, lakes and rivers, baseball fields, or tennis courts. For those looking to walk, hike, or bike, trails are also marked on park maps.

St. Paul, Minnesota, is home to the Como Park Zoo and Conservatory. It's not just your ordinary zoo and garden—it has everything from arts and crafts and concerts to mini golf!

# Arts and Culture

Museums. Cultural centers. Famous buildings. Monuments and historical sites. Theaters and concert halls. These things make cities fun and interesting places to live and visit. City planners create special maps to make sure people can find all of these amazing sites.

## Paris, France

Paris, nicknamed the "City of Light," is located along the River Seine in northern France. This historic city is famous for its music, art, architecture, and food. More than 2 million people call this French capital home, and nearly 20 million people visit every year. They visit places including the Eiffel Tower, the Louvre Museum, and Notre Dame Cathedral.

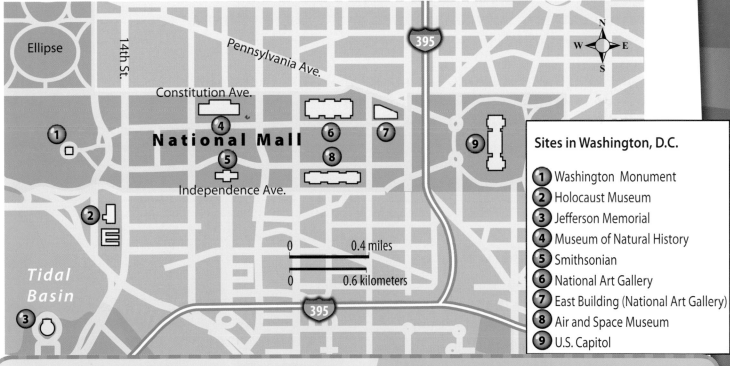

**Sites in Washington, D.C.**

1. Washington Monument
2. Holocaust Museum
3. Jefferson Memorial
4. Museum of Natural History
5. Smithsonian
6. National Art Gallery
7. East Building (National Art Gallery)
8. Air and Space Museum
9. U.S. Capitol

## Map It! A Trip to the Mall

The National Mall is located in the center of Washington, D.C. It is surrounded by many monuments, museums, and gardens, and it spreads across more than 1,000 acres (4 km²).

## Read It!

The buildings and monuments are marked on the map and in the key. If you want to go from the Museum of Natural History to the U.S. Capitol, which roads would you take? What sites could you see along the way?

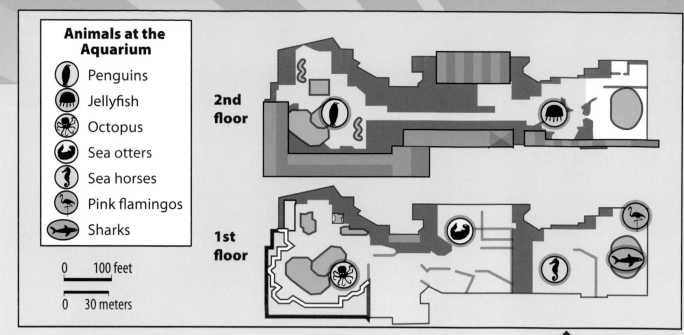

## Animals at the Aquarium

- 🐧 Penguins
- 🪼 Jellyfish
- 🐙 Octopus
- 🦦 Sea otters
- 🌊 Sea horses
- 🦩 Pink flamingos
- 🦈 Sharks

2nd floor

1st floor

0    100 feet

0    30 meters

# Find It!

Finding your destination is just the first step. Once you're there, you need to know what the place has to offer and how to get around. Whether you're at a museum, an amusement park, a national park, or a castle, you'll find a map that will show you where everything is located and how to get there. Some maps even show where restaurants, shops, information centers, and restrooms are located.

People use these maps to plan their visits and make sure they see everything they came for. Without a map, they'd just be wandering around. And some places are so big, they'd probably get lost!

This aquarium is huge and has a lot of exhibits. Luckily, the map shows where each exhibit is located. You just saw feeding time at the penguin enclosure, and now you want to watch the sharks swim. How do you get to the shark tank?

## Did You Know?

Times Square in New York City is the most-visited site in the world. More than 35 million people stand on the street staring at these neon signs every year.

# Activity

## A Day at the Park

### Materials
- map of an amusement park (provided)
- pencil

Amusement parks have maps to help visitors find their way from one ride to another. Restaurants, restrooms, and shops are also marked. Use the map to find your way around the park.

1. Photocopy the map below. Then follow the instructions to draw your route.

2. You want to go on the roller coaster first. Which way do you turn at the entrance?

3. The haunted house sounds fun, but so does the log ride. How do you do both with the least amount of walking?

4. You and your friend decide to try the bouncy castle. How do you get there?

5. It's almost time for lunch. Can you find the restaurant?

6. While eating, you are asked to go to the help desk. They've found your wallet. How do you get there?

7. You and your friend want to go on the bumper cars. You decide to stop at the restrooms first. Is it a long walk?

8. You want a picture to remember this fun day. Where is the photo booth?

9. It's almost time to leave. Your mom is waiting to pick you up at the entrance. What is the fastest way to get there?

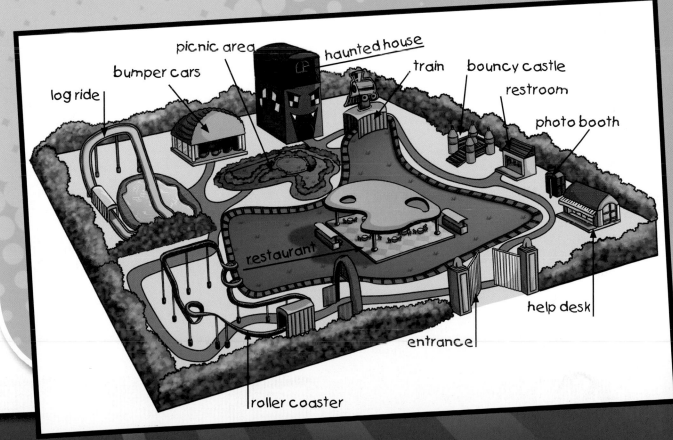

# The Future Cities

Many cities are overcrowded and polluted and use up too many natural resources. Some city planners are looking for ways to solve these problems.

Planners are designing cities that rely on solar power and environmentally friendly materials. Their plans will change the way we live, work, and get around.

**GOING GREEN**
The buildings in the plan for the Gwanggyo Power Centre in South Korea look like hills and hives. The materials used to build them are extremely environmentally friendly. More than 75,000 people could live and work in a relatively small area.

**MOON TOWN**
The National Aeronautics and Space Administration (NASA) has announced plans to build a permanent base for people on the Moon in the year 2020.

# Majestic Cities

Cites are amazing and exciting places.
Here are a few more fascinating facts!

- New York City is home to nine professional sports teams.

- Berlin, Germany, used to be divided by a concrete wall. One half was part of East Germany, the other West Germany.

- People from more than 140 countries live in Los Angeles, California. More than 220 languages are spoken there.

- Before 1945, less that 40 percent of people lived in suburbs. By 2000, that number had jumped to more than 77 percent!

- Every building in Yakutsk, Russia, is built on stilts. That's because the ground in Yakutsk—the world's coldest city—is permafrost, or frozen soil.

- Houston, Texas, is home to NASA's Johnson Space Center where the Mission Control Center is located.

- Hum, Croatia, is the world's smallest town. Fewer than 25 people live there!

# Glossary

**agriculture** The planned planting and harvesting of crops.

**boroughs** Smaller parts of a city.

**commute** To travel back and forth between work and home.

**culture** The history, traditions, arts, and practices of a specific nation or group of people.

**deposits** Large amounts of natural resources, such as minerals, in the ground.

**developers** People who build on or change an area.

**downtown** The main business area of a city or town.

**elevated** Raised above the ground.

**evacuation** Moving people quickly away from an area in danger.

**exhibit** Public display in a museum, art gallery, fair, or zoo.

**fertile** Able to produce or grow.

**filter** Remove harmful or poisonous substances.

**financial hub** Center of banking and business.

**monuments** Structures that honor a person or event.

**navigate** To find or plan a route from one place to another.

**population density** The number of people per square mile or square kilometer.

**products** Items sold to consumers.

**property line** A line on a map between areas of land that are owned by different people.

**satellites** Human-made machines that orbit Earth; used to collect information or for communication.

**suburb** Outlying community of a city.

**townships** Smaller parts of a city, usually with their own governments.

**utilities** Services provided by a city, such as electricity, gas, and water.

**wards** Sections of a city or borough.

**zoned** Areas of land designated for a specific purpose or use.

# To Learn More

## Books

Bodden, Valerie. *A Suburb*. Mankato, MN: Creative Education, 2008. Easy-to-follow text and photographs bring readers into the modern suburb.

Scholl, Elizabeth. *Class Trip: New York City*. Hockessin, DE: Mitchell Lane Publishers, 2010. Come along on a class trip to New York City! Learn all about the city's history and places of interest.

Sperling, Bert, and Peter Sander. *Cities Ranked and Rated*. Hoboken, NJ: Wiley Publishing, Inc., 2007. More than 400 metropolitan areas are reviewed and graded in this interesting title.

## Websites

**http://kids.dc.gov/kids_main_content.html**
A fun and easy online resource for learning about our nation's capitol. The colorful interface will interest children of all ages.

**http://travel.nationalgeographic.com/places/cities/index.html**
Learn about the different cities around the world. Click on any city to find images, maps, articles, and fascinating facts.

**http://myminicity.com**
Visitors can go online and make a city of their very own! Be in charge of the buildings, trees, and all the other features that make up a city.

# Index